This Boxer Books paperback belongs to

. . . .

www.boxerbooks.com

For my Nan who understands
H.B.

In memory of my friend Sanja Rudic
M.S.

Consultant:
Paul S. Littlewood BSc(Hons), MSc
Fellow of the Royal Geographical Society Scientific Fellow of the Zoological Society of London

This paperback edition published in 2007

First published in Great Britain in 2007 by Boxer Books Limited www.boxerbooks.com

Hardback ISBN 10: 1-905417-35-7
Hardback ISBN 13: 978-1-905417-35-3
Paperback ISBN 13: 978-1-905417-42-1

1 3 5 7 9 10 8 6 4 2

Printed in China

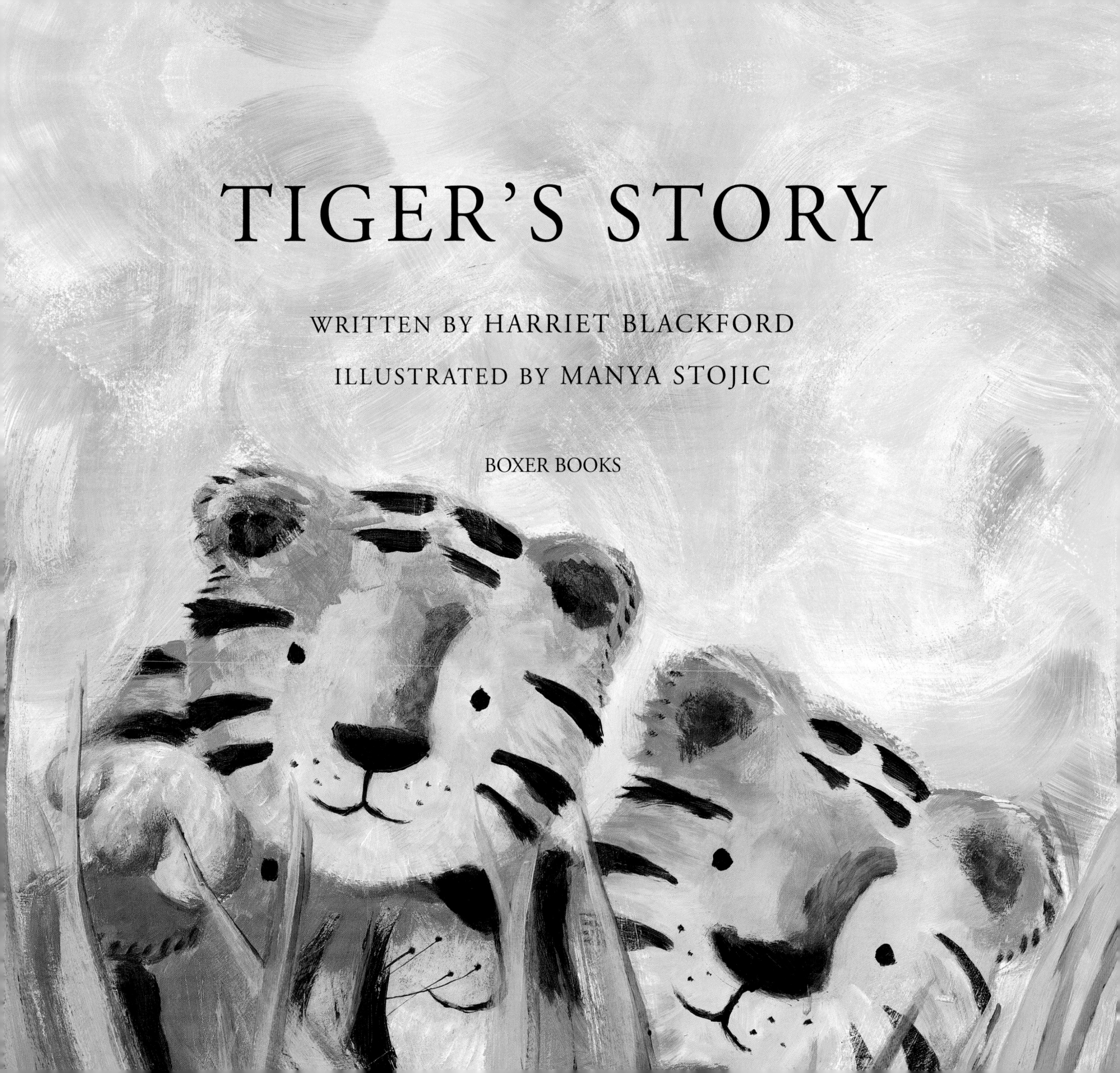

TIGER'S STORY

WRITTEN BY HARRIET BLACKFORD

ILLUSTRATED BY MANYA STOJIC

BOXER BOOKS

Tiger is a small, strong, stripey cub.
He lives with his mother and sisters
in a forest in India. He walks quietly
on his big soft paws and twitches his
long stripey tail.

Tiger's favourite thing to do is crouch down low in the tall grass, where his stripes make him seem to disappear. Then suddenly Tiger pounces on his sisters, and they all roll around and tumble together.

Tiger knows all the sights, sounds and smells of his forest home. Monkeys chatter in the trees and butterflies flutter near the stream. The tiger cubs are growing up fast.

Soon they are old enough to go hunting with their mother. Sometimes Tiger catches his own dinner. It's a very small dinner so he doesn't have to share!

Tiger is getting older and growing bigger.
He is so good at hunting now that he goes
exploring on his own for days at a time—over
the hill, across the stream and along the path
that runs through the tall grass.

When Tiger comes home,
his mother greets him.
He is almost as big
as she is now!

Tiger doesn't visit his mother and sisters very often any more. One day, Tiger knows that he needs his own space to hunt. So Tiger sets off on a long journey, far away from his mother, far away from the hill and the stream and the path that runs though the grass.

When Tiger comes to a new part of the forest, his sense of smell tells him that deer have just passed by. Wild pigs have walked in the tall grass. But what's this?

Another tiger's smell.
This tiger doesn't smell like
Tiger's mother or his sisters.

Then he sees it. A great big grown-up tiger, twitching his long stripey tail and staring straight at Tiger. Tiger stands very still.

He sniffs the tiger smell again. He is not sure what he should do. But he does know that he must be VERY quiet.

Tiger freezes. He knows he shouldn't be here in this other tiger's territory. The other tiger creeps towards him. Suddenly Tiger turns, and he runs and runs and runs!

After a while, Tiger stops running. He sniffs the air.
He is sure there's no smell of that big angry tiger in
this new place.

Tiger is a long way from home.
The sun is shining through the trees and noisy
monkeys chatter overhead. Just like in his old home,
there is a stream nearby with fluttering butterflies.

Tiger can see deer up ahead in the tall grass.

This new part of the forest is a good place
for Tiger. He is old enough to take care of himself
now. To warn other tigers that he lives here he
spreads his own smell around the bushes and trees.
Tiger washes his paws with his rough pink tongue
and curls up for a nap. It is good to be home.

Tigers

A note from the author

Tigers learn to look after themselves as they grow up, just as children do, but tigers grow up much faster than children. This book tells a story about one particular young tiger and how he grew up.

First, here are some facts about tigers. Tigers are one of the world's biggest wild cats. A male tiger can weigh as much as four grown-up people. Tigers are found in India, parts of China, Russia (far eastern) and Southeast Asia. They live in a variety of places, or habitats: tropical forests, tall grasslands, mixed forests and mangrove swamps.

Tigers have black stripes on their orange fur, which makes them hard to see in the forests and tall grass. This is called camouflage and it helps them to hide while they are hunting for food. Tigers hunt deer and wild pigs to eat and they also catch smaller animals.

A female tiger is all grown up and starts to have babies when she is about four years old. She usually has two or three babies at a time. The babies are called cubs. They live with their mother for eighteen months to just over two years before they gradually move away and find homes of their own.

Tigers live in an area called a territory, which they can defend against other tigers. They spray a mixture of urine and scent on to trees, grass, bushes and rocks so other tigers will know that someone is already living there.

Tigers are an endangered species. This means that there are very few wild tigers left in the world. In the past, they were hunted for sport, for their fur and by people who used their bones for traditional medicines. Today, while hunting has been banned, tigers are still killed and this is called poaching.

People are also destroying the tigers' habitats by cutting down forests and putting up buildings in their territories. Tigers need to eat a lot of animals. In places where their territory is shrinking, there are not enough animals (prey) left for them to hunt for food. People who care about tigers are trying very hard to stop the poaching and building in the tigers' habitats. They want to make it possible for tigers to go on living in the wild. One day perhaps you too can help save the tigers.

Other Boxer Books paperbacks

Big Smelly Bear: Britta Teckentrup
Big Smelly Bear never washed, brushed or took
a bath. Big Smelly Bear was followed by a big
smelly stink, wherever he went. Can his new-
found friend persuade him to take a bath?
ISBN13: 978-1-905417-43-8

I Love My Mummy: Sebastien Braun
Sometimes parents are loud and playful.
Sometimes they are quiet and compassionate.
And they are always loving.
Shortlisted - Best New Illustrator 2006
BOOKTRUST EARLY YEARS AWARDS
ISBN13: 978-0-9547373-6-8

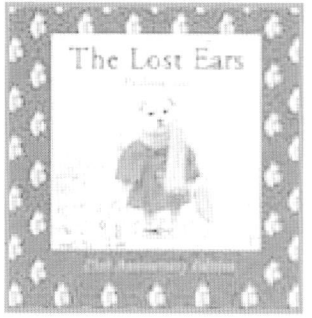

The Lost Ears: Phillida Gili
Once upon a time there lived a teddy called
Harry, who was only two and a half inches tall.
Then one day something completely unexpected
happened to him...
TWENTY-FIFTH ANNIVERSARY EDITION
ISBN13: 978-1-905417-44-5

Little Smudge: Lionel Le Néouanic
"Hello.
Could I play with you ?"
A simple, elegant and innovative tale about
the importance of mixing, making friends
and appreciating differences.
ISBN13: 978-1-905417-23-0